TECHNOLOGY
INVENTORS

by
Rebecca Phillips-Bartlett

Minneapolis, Minnesota

Credits

All images are courtesy of Shutterstock.com, unless otherwise specified. With thanks to Getty Images, Thinkstock Photo, and iStockphoto.

Recurring images – Andrew Rybalko, cosmaa, andromina, P-fotography, Mark Rademaker, vectorlab2D, Designsells. Cover – Andrew Rybalko, dimair, cosmaa, andromina, P-fotography, vectorlab2D, StrongPickles. 2–3 – VectorShow. 4–5 – Designsells, Ground Picture, Natalllenka.m. 6–7 – Jiang Zhongyan, Marish, Malika Keehl, Natalllenka.m, изображение_viber. 8–9 – Wikimedia Commons/Public Domain, Jan Schneckenhaus, Oxy_gen, StrongPickles, Morphart Creation. 10–11 – Procy, GoodStudio. 12–13 – Paul Maguire, Abscent Vector, Pogorelova Olga, Roi and Roi. 14–15 – Crisco 1492, GOLDMAN99, ST.art, Inactive design, vectorlab2D. 16–17 – Light show, WEB-DESIGN, beboy. 18–19 – Wikimedia Commons/Public Domain, svekloid, GOLDMAN99, robuart, Onica Alexandru Sergiu, Cuteness here. 20–21 – BRO.vector, Wikimedia Commons/Public Domain, Sergio Andres Segovia, Vanatchanan, d1sk, notbad, Sudowoodo, Paulrclarke. 22–23 – MillaF, GoodStudio, Designsells.

Library of Congress Cataloging-in-Publication Data

Names: Phillips-Bartlett, Rebecca, 1999- author.
Title: Technology inventors / Rebecca Phillips-Bartlett.
Description: Minneapolis, Minnesota : Bearport Publishing Company, [2024] |
  Series: Brilliant people, big ideas | Includes index.
Identifiers: LCCN 2023030972 (print) | LCCN 2023030973 (ebook) | ISBN
  9798889163589 (library binding) | ISBN 9798889163633 (paperback) | ISBN
  9798889163671 (ebook)
Subjects: LCSH: Inventions--Juvenile literature. | Inventors--Juvenile
  literature. | Technological innovations--Juvenile literature.
Classification: LCC T48 .P493 2024 (print) | LCC T48 (ebook) | DDC
  609.2--dc23/eng/20230711
LC record available at https://lccn.loc.gov/2023030972
LC ebook record available at https://lccn.loc.gov/2023030973

© 2024 BookLife Publishing
This edition is published by arrangement with BookLife Publishing.

North American adaptations © 2024 Bearport Publishing Company. All rights reserved. No part of this publication may be reproduced in whole or in part, stored in any retrieval system, or transmitted in any form or by any means, electronic, mechanical, photocopying, recording, or otherwise, without written permission from the publisher.

For more information, write to Bearport Publishing, 5357 Penn Avenue South, Minneapolis, MN 55419.

Contents

Big Ideas...................... 4

Li Tian 6

Johannes Gutenberg............. 8

Alexander Graham Bell 10

Alice H. Parker 12

Grace Hopper.................. 14

Hedy Lamarr.................. 16

Gerald "Jerry" A. Lawson 18

The Hall of Fame 20

All You Need Is an Idea! 22

Glossary..................... 24

Index 24

Big Ideas

Today, we can solve many problems using **technology**. But do you know about the people who first made these problem-solving machines possible?

From fireworks to telephones, who do we have to thank for these amazing **inventions**? It was scientists and inventors who turned big ideas into **brilliant** inventions.

What tech do you use every day?

5

Li Tian

"Firecrackers are not only for celebrating...."

AROUND 601 CE–690 CE

Firecrackers

Li Tian may have invented the first firecracker. Stories say he put **gunpowder** into a bamboo stick and threw the stick into a fire. *Pow!* People thought the loud noise would scare away evil **spirits**!

When have you seen fireworks?

Soon, people used the same idea to make fireworks. Today, we celebrate many important days, such as Diwali and the 4th of July, with these bursts of color.

Johannes Gutenberg

You would not be reading this book without me....

AROUND 1400–1468

Printing Press

Johannes Gutenberg invented the printing press. This machine made it easy to print many copies of the same book. Before this invention, most books were written by hand.

How long do you think it would take to write your favorite book by hand?

Books written by hand cost lots of money, so only rich people could have them. Today, everybody has books to read!

Alexander Graham Bell

No one thought my invention would be possible!

1847–1922

Telephone

More than 100 years ago, most people wrote letters to send messages far away. Then, Alexander Graham Bell and Thomas Watson invented a machine that could send a voice through a wire.

Soon, people could use this machine to speak to others far away. Alexander called this invention the electrical speech machine. Today, we call it a phone.

Most phones today are wireless.

Alice H. Parker

During the winter, my house was way too cold! Then, I had an idea....

AROUND 1895–1920

Central Heating

A hundred years ago, people had to collect wood or **coal** to heat their homes. They burned it to make fire. Alice Parker invented a heater that could warm up houses using gas instead.

Using gas saves time from gathering and chopping wood.

Today, Alice's invention is called central heating. It is safer than lighting a fire in every room of your house!

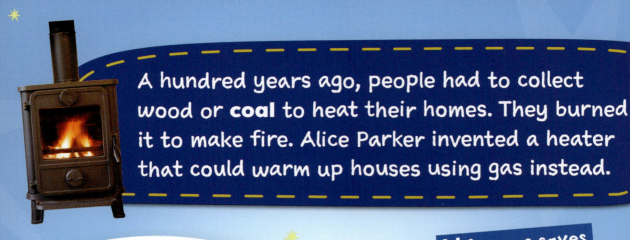

Grace Hopper

I invented a new way for computers to work!

1906–1992

Computer Programming

Early computers used numbers and symbols to do work. But it was a confusing language. People needed to learn what those numbers were saying if they wanted to use computers.

Grace Hopper was a rear admiral for the U.S. Navy.

Grace invented a way to make computers understand words along with numbers and symbols. This made it easier for people to use computers.

15

Hedy Lamarr was a famous **actor**. But she was also an amazing inventor! Hedy invented tech that made Wi-Fi work.

Today, we use Wi-Fi for many different things. We can use it to play games or do homework on a tablet.

What do you use Wi-Fi for?

Gerald "Jerry" A. Lawson

My invention let people play video games at home.

1940–2011

Video Game Cartridges

Early video games could only be played at arcades. People had to put coins into big machines that were shared by everybody at the arcade.

Arcade machine

What is your favorite video game?

Jerry Lawson invented **cartridges**, which let people play many games on a single machine. This made it possible for people to play games at home, too.

The Hall of Fame

Here are some more brilliant people who deserve a place in our technology hall of fame.

John Harrington

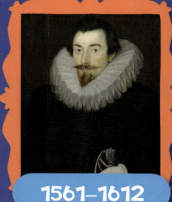

1561–1612

John Harrington invented the flush toilet. Imagine the smell before he came up with his idea!

Sir Tim Berners-Lee

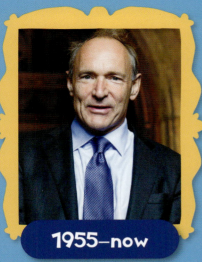

Sir Tim Berners-Lee invented the World Wide Web. We also call this the internet.

1955–now

Ajay Bhatt

Ajay Bhatt invented USB cables. They can connect and charge today's tech.

1957–now

All You Need Is an Idea!

All these inventions started the same way. They were big ideas. From book printing to Wi-Fi, a lot of our favorite tech wouldn't be the same without brilliant people.

Glossary

actor a person who acts on stage, on TV, or in the movies

brilliant extremely smart

cartridges small containers that can be swapped out in a machine to play different video games

coal a solid fuel that is found in the ground

gunpowder a black powder that explodes easily

inventions new things that have been made to solve problems

spirits supernatural beings, such as ghosts

technology the use of science to invent useful tools

Index

books 8–9, 22
central heating 12–13
computers 14–15
fire 7, 13
firecrackers 6–7
internet 21–22

letters 11
printing press 8–9
technology 4–5, 17, 20–23
telephones 5, 10–11
USB 21
Wi-Fi 16–17, 22